Where's Duke?

Written By Daniel Urshan

Illustrations by Aurora Webster

Visit WheresDuke.com for a free coloring page!

Authors Note:

I will never be able to thank the team at Animal Allies enough for providing medical attention to "Old Duke" when he was lost. I had always dreamed of creating something to give back and thank them for their efforts. Today, I am happy to say that I did. Although this is a true story that I retell to my grandchildren often, this book was specifically written as a fundraising tool with proceeds going to Animal Allies. My hope is that benefits from this project will help them both now and for many years in the future.

Thank you for your contribution to this dream.
Dan Urshan, Author

ISBN 978-1-7328782-0-4

Copyright©2018 by Daniel Urshan
All rights reserved. Published by Lake Superior Marketing LLC 5119 Cedar Ridge Dr Duluth, MN 55811, by arrangement with Daniel Urshan.

Printed in the USA

For more information visit: WheresDuke.com

Dedicated to my grandchildren:
Isla Pearl
Maeylin Lu
Emmaline Lee
Ezekiel Benjamin
Andre Daniel

Special thanks to:
My wife, Cindy and my children, Andrea and Jordan for your love and support.
My mom and dad for being the best parents Danny could've asked for.
My brother Davey for being a great brother.
Mr. Jackson for being a good neighbor and taking such good care of Duke.
Shawna Jokinen at Lake Superior Marketing for helping me make this dream into reality.
Aurora Webster for your skill and dedication to getting the job done.
Thank you all for your unwavering support.
-Dan

"Hey Duke! Fetch!"
Danny had a black Labrador puppy named Duke. Duke loved
retrieving sticks and balls from the water.
He also loved playing and wrestling with Danny and his brother
Davey in the yard.

Duke followed the brothers everywhere they went and would even sneak in and snuggle with them at night.

As Duke got older, the boys would take Duke hunting and fishing with them. He was a great dog and a loved member of the family.

When Danny was at school during the day, Duke would spend time with their neighbor, Mr. Jackson. Mr. Jackson adored Duke and would take Duke on special walks around the neighborhood to visit all the other neighbors in the area. Then he and Duke would go back and spend their afternoons napping in Mr. Jackson's living room. Mr. Jackson would fall asleep in his rocking chair and Duke would sleep on the floor beside him. They were quite a pair! Mr. Jackson loved having a friend to keep him company during the day.

One day, Danny noticed that Duke was missing.
He wasn't at home or at Mr. Jackson's house. He couldn't be found anywhere in the neighborhood. Duke was gone!
Danny asked Mr. Jackson to help him call for the dog.
"Heyyyy Duuuke!", Mr. Jackson called. "Where are you?!"

Danny's family looked everywhere for Duke with no luck.
The family put up signs.... they put an ad in the newspaper.... and then
they placed a radio ad to try and find him. It seemed like everyone
was on the lookout for Old Duke! The local television station had
even tried to help by broadcasting a lost dog announcement.

They got a phone call one day… Someone had seen a black dog on a nearby street. Excitedly, Danny's family hurried to go look for the dog but when they got there it was not Duke.
It was just another black dog.

Danny's mom sat down to
have talk with the boys after about a month of searching...
"I want you to know how proud I am that you boys have never
given up and have never stopped looking for Duke," Danny's mom
said," But you have to understand that Duke may never come home."

Danny began to cry. "Where's Duke?," he sobbed.
"He has to be somewhere!"
Danny felt terrible that he could not find his dog. He didn't even
get the chance to say goodbye. He didn't know what he would do
without his dog. Duke was his best friend!

About twenty miles away...

A family in the next town over
spotted dog tracks going into
their old barn.

When they went to investigate....
They found a very skinny, weak black Labrador sitting in a pile of hay. He was so cold and hungry that he could barely walk.

The family knew that the dog needed help so they brought him inside the house as quickly as they could to give him food and water.

The dog was missing his collar and tags so the family had no clue who he belonged to. The family knew lost dogs should be turned in to an animal shelter if their owners could not be found.

They contacted Animal Allies, the animal shelter in their town, and brought the dog in.

After arriving at Animal Allies, the black Labrador was brought to the local Veterinary clinic to get the care he needed.

A dog trainer named Joe was at the clinic when the dog came in. Joe was almost sure he had seen the dog before but he couldn't quite remember who the dog belonged to.

Danny's family also owned a litter of puppies at this time. They had to bring one of the puppies in to the Veterinarian Clinic for shots and just missed seeing Duke with the caretaker from Animal Allies. He had left just before they got there.

While searching for Duke's family, Animal Allies allowed the black Labrador to be placed in another home with a loving family who would take care of him until his owners could be found.

He was such a good dog that they fell in love with him immediately.

The family did not know the dog's name so they had to come up with something new. They chose to name him "Super Dog" because he was making such a great recovery.

Duke continued to get stronger every day!

News travels in a small town and eventually, a friend of Danny's heard about "Super Dog."

Hmm...he wondered.

Could this "Super Dog" really be Duke?

He called Danny's parents and told Danny's mom about the dog that had been found in the next town over.

Danny's mom didn't tell her boys about the call because she didn't want them to be disappointed if it turned out to be a different lost dog again. While the kids were at school, she drove out to see if Duke had really be found.

When Danny's mom got to "Super Dog's" house, she walked out into the yard and exclaimed, "Duke! It's you!"

Duke got up and raced over to Danny's mom!
"We've never seen him get up so fast!" exclaimed the homeowner
"We definitely know he's your dog!"
The homeowners were really going to miss him but they were happy that Duke could go back to his family.

Danny's mom was so relieved! She couldn't wait to show the boys!

When Danny and his brother Davey got home from school, their mom said excitedly, "Boys…. There's an old friend in the living room who wants to see you!"

The boys ran into the living room and when they saw Duke, their eyes widened with surprise! They couldn't believe it!
They cried with delight and couldn't stop hugging him!
Their best friend was back!
The boys knew that their neighbor, Mr. Jackson was probably missing Duke as much as they had. They just had to bring Old Duke over to see him. Mr. Jackson would be thrilled!

The whole family walked over to surprise Mr. Jackson.
Danny and Davey waited outside with Duke...

Danny's father went up to the door to knock and said, "Mr. Jackson!
You have someone outside who wants to see you!"

"Well, bring them inside!" Mr. Jackson's voice called from inside the
house. The boys let Duke gallop into the house!

Mr. Jackson was in disbelief! After being gone for two months, Duke
was happily charging towards him. He was so happy that he cried
tears of joy as Duke licked his face!

When news got out that Duke had been found, the whole neighborhood cheered. Duke's story even ended up making the front page of the local newspaper!

Danny had never been so happy. He spent the rest of the summer playing fetch with Duke and joining Mr. Jackson and Duke on their daily walks around the neighborhood.

About Author Daniel Urshan

Daniel "Danny" Urshan grew up on Big Grand Lake in the town of Twig, just 10 miles north of Duluth, MN. He spent his summers swimming in the lake and helping the family raise young Labrador pups. Danny's family loved all animals, but they really loved their dogs!

In the mid 1960's the Urshan family had a young black Labrador pup named Duke that would become a member of their family and a best friend to the Urshan kids. Everyone loved Duke. Even neighbor Mr. David Jackson, a widower, took a liking to him and forged a lifelong friendship with both Duke and the Urshan family.

Danny now goes by the name Dan and is married to his wife Cindy of 34 years. Together they have two children and five grandchildren. In Dan's spare time he likes to spend time with his family and friends, retelling some of his childhood stories. His grandchildren love it! One of their favorites is the "Where's Duke?" story about the time when Duke went missing. This story has been told countless times along with many of Dan's other childhood adventures.

When Dan isn't spending time with family and friends he stays busy running his business and helping with community causes. Dan has been in business for 34 years, is a former city councilman and has a two-term mayor in Hermantown MN. In 1998, Dan (Mayor Urshan) also received the American Hometown Leadership Award for "highest standards of dedication, ability, creativity and leadership in local government" from the National Center for Small Communities. Dan is thrilled to be an active member of his community and looks forward to serving for many years to come.

For more information visit: WheresDuke.com

Mission Statement

Animal Allies Humane Society strives to ensure a loving home for every pet.

Organization History

Animal Allies Humane Society was founded in the 1950s when a Duluth school teacher, Miriam Carlstedt, took responsibility of caring for and finding homes for a litter of kittens she discovered on her doorstep. She dedicated herself to animal welfare, introducing humane education programs to area schools and developing a network of volunteers to foster and find homes for homeless companion animals. Animal Allies was incorporated in 1957 and later gained 501c3 status in February, 1968.

Animal Allies operated out of homes until the late 1990s when they partnered with the City of Duluth Animal Services, sharing their facility and performing all adoption services for the city's homeless pets. From 2007-2008, donors and supporters contributed to Animal Allies' capital campaign to build the new, state-of-the-art shelter that they operate from currently today.

Support Future Life-Saving Efforts at Animal Allies:
www.animalallies.net/donate